For information about special discounts available for
bulk purchases, sales promotions, fund-raising and
educational needs, contact us at
TAROTAROMEDIA@gmail.com

Title ID: 6041782
ISBN-13: 978-1523827602

READY?

(1) IT WAS THE NORWEGIANS WHO
INTRODUCED 'SALMON SUSHI' TO THE Japanese

Japan had not imported a single piece of fish or had the habit of consuming raw salmon until the 1970's. This project, which was an attempt to promote the exportation of Norwegian seafood, turned out to be a great success and today norwegian salmon is the most popular fish of choice among young Japanese.

(2) KAITEN ZUSHI

is where various Sushi dishes are placed on a conveyor belt and customers pick up the ones they want and each plate has a different color or even rfid tags/barcodes, according to their price.

California Rolls are

MADE

INSIDE OUT

because Westerners did not
like the texture of seaweed
covering the rolls.

(4) Originally, Sushi was made by wrapping fish in soured fermenting rice, and ONLY THE FISH WAS TAKEN OUT AND CONSUMED – this is known as 'NAREZUSHI'.

(5) Traditionally, SUSHI IS EATEN WITH HANDS.

(6) When enjoying Sushi, it should be TURNED OVER so that only the topping is dipped in soy sauce.

すし

(7) The most expensive Sushi was made by a Filipino chef Angelito Araneta Jr. - It was wrapped in gold leaf, topped with caviar, three Mikimoto pearls, and served with a diamond. IT WAS PRICED AT $1,978.15 USD.

(8) Sushi used to be STREET FOOD SOLD ON MOBILE FOOD STALLS, made of an oblong mound of rice and a slice of fish covered on top.

(9) When contemporary Sushi was first introduced by Hanaya Yohei, the size of Sushi was about THREE TIMES BIGGER than they are now.

(10) 'INARIZUSHI', a pouch of fried tofu filled with rice, is NAMED AFTER THE Shinto GOD, INARI, who's believed to love fried tofu.

(11) Sweet pickled ginger, 'GARI', is consumed between Sushi courses TO CLEANSE THE PALATE AND HELP DIGESTION.

(12) 'GARI', is actually pale yellow in color and is OFTEN DYED PINK with an artificial coloring agent or beet juice.

(13) Those green plastic grass in takeout sushi is called 'BARAN', and they PREVENT THE FLAVORS OF ADJACENT PIECES OF SUSHI FROM MIXING UP.

(14) Before plastic grass, real leaves from cast iron plant and sasa bamboo were used and their antimicrobial phytoncides EXTENDED THE SHELF LIFE OF SUSHI.

(15) Japanese Sashimi (fish fillet) knives are SHARPENED ONLY ON ONE SIDE because it is believed to cut better and make cleaner cuts, but it requires more skills.

(16) The term 'Sushi' originates from an ancient grammatical form that's no longer used, and it means "SOUR TASTING".

(17) Only highly trained and licensed chefs are allowed to prepare 'FUGU', or blowfish, because it contains tetrodoxtrin which could cause serious harm, even death –

This is why it is

THE ONLY FOOD

THE JAPANESE EMPEROR IS FORBIDDEN TO EAT.

(18) Since 2000, **23 PEOPLE HAVE DIED FROM EATING FUGU** in Japan

Mt. FUJI

(19) The first person to climb Mt. Fuji was a monk whose name is still not known until today.

(20) There are Japanese Self-Defense Forces and the United States marine corps military bases near Mt. Fuji that are still being operated.

(21) Until the Meiji era, women were allowed to the summit of Mt. Fuji because it was considered a sacred place.

(22) The logo of the Japanese automobile company, Infiniti, was inspired by Mt. Fuji.

(24) Approximately 300,000 people climbed Mt. Fuji in 2009.

(23) The first foreigner to ascend the summit was by Sir Rutherford Alcock in 1868, and it took him 8 hours to reach the top but only 3 hours to come back down.

(25) Lady Fanny Parkes, the wife of a British ambassador was the first foreign woman to climb the summit of Mt. Fuji.

(26) Ancient Samurai used the base of Mt. Fuji as a training area.

(27) Influenced by Buddhist concept of reincarnation and rebirth, some Samurai gave up violence and became monks.

(28) For Samurai, a wife's failure to produce a son was an acceptable cause for divorce but adopting a male heir was a way to avoid it.

(29) William Adams (1564-1620), an English sailor and adventurer, was the first Westerner to receive the Samurai dignity.

(30) Today, over 90% of all adoptions are of adult males in their 20's and 30's – the main reason is to secure a familial heir.

(31) In Spain, there are people with the surname 'Japon' who are descendants of 17th century samurais that originally came to the small town of Coria del Rio as part of a Japanese delegation and stayed on.

SAMURAI

(32) 'Seppuku', a way of committing suicide by cutting abdomen, was part of the Samurai honor code of dying with honor before falling to the hands of their enemies.

"Ukiyo-e woodblock print of warrior about to perform seppuku" by Kunikazu Utagawa

It was also a capital punishment for those who committed serious offenses or brought shame to themselves.

(33) The first specialized training of Ninja began in the mid-15th century when some samurai families started practicing covert warfare.

(34) Contrary to popular belief, Ninja did not always work alone and there were various teamwork techniques such as climbing a high wall using each other as a platform.

(35) Ninja threw duckweed over water to conceal underwater movement.

(36) Common Ninja disguises include priests, entertainers, fortune tellers, merchants, and monks.

(37) Unlike today's image of Ninja wearing black garb, it was much more common for them to be disguised as civilians.

(38) Some Ninja legends include the ability to fly, become invisible, shape shift and split into multiple bodies.

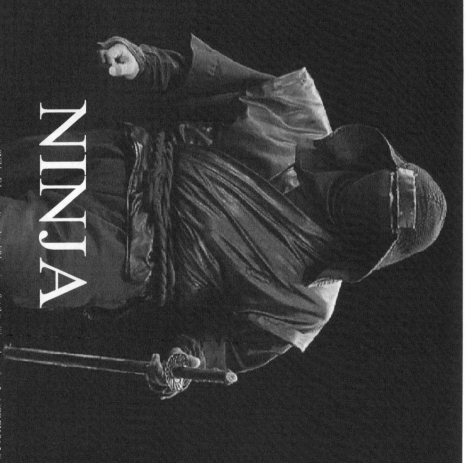

NINJA

(39) Katana sword, one of many weapons of Samurai, needed to be polished by an experienced master, because improper polishing would ruin the blade completely.

(40) Bladesmithing was held in such high regard, a smith would often fast, engage in abstinence, and even go on a pilgrimage before beginning his work.

(41) The most expensive Katana sword a 13th century 'KAMAKURA' blade which was sold for $418,000 USD to an anonymous European collector.

(42) The reason why 'GENDAITO', handmade 'SHINKEN (real swords)' are so expensive, often starting at $6,000 USD for the blade alone, is because the swordsmiths are limited by the Japanese law to produce no more than 24 swords per year.

(43) Sumo has its roots in Shinto (ethnic Japanese religion) rituals used to ensure a rich harvest and honor the spirits known as 'KAMI'.

(44) Although trying to maintain and keep their traditions, Sumo is open to foreign players, and there have been numerous top wrestlers who even reached 'YOKOZUNA', the champion of Sumo.

(45) No women are allowed to enter a Sumo ring as it's considered a violation of purity, and for this reason a female governor of Osaka could not enter the ring to award the winner at their annual Sumo tournament.

(46) The role of the Sumo officiator resembles that of a Shinto priest, and the act of throwing salt before a match fis to purify the ring by chasing away evil spirits.

(47) There is a 400-year tradition of 'CRYING SUMO (NAKI ZUMO)' contest in Japan which takes place at the sensoji temple in Tokyo every year. Sumo wrestlers hold babies and encourage them to cry – it is rooted in the belief that babies crying chases evil sprits away and brings in good health. Whoever cries first wins the prize, but in case of many, the one that cries the loudest becomes the winner.

(48) The greater Tokyo area, consisted of the Kanto region, the Tokyo metropolis, and the prefecture of Yamanashi, is the most heavily populated metropolitan area in the world – in 2014, the estimated population for the area was 37,832,892, which is more people than that of canada or iraq.

(50) Originally, Tokyo was a small fishing village named 'Edo'.

(51) The Safe City Index ranked Tokyo as the safest city in the world.

(52) During World War II, more than half of Tokyo was destroyed and the population dropped from 6,700,000 to 2,800,000.

(54) With a total GDP of $1.9 Trillion USD, Tokyo has the largest metropolitan economy in the world.

(55) Tokyo Joe, Tokyo Story, My Geisha, Ou Only Live Twice, Kill Bill, Fast And The Furious: Tokyo Drift, Lost In Translation, Babel, Inception are some of the famous Hollywood movies featuring Tokyo as a backdrop.

(56) Tokyo means "eastern capital" in Japanese.

(57) Tokyo is the only Asian city to host the summer Olympic Games twice – in 1964 and again in 2020.

(53) Five of the world's top 25 most visited theme parks are in Japan. Tokyo disneyland, Tokyo Disney Sea, Universal Studios in Osaka, Nagashima Spa Land, Mie prefecture, and Yokohama Sea Paradise.

(49) Tokyo has the most number of Michelin star restaurants (229) in the world, surpassing Paris(94).

(58) 36% Of Tokyo is covered by forest.

TOKYO

(59) Measuring 634 meters (2080 feet) tall, 'TOKYO SKYTREE' is the tallest communications tower in the world

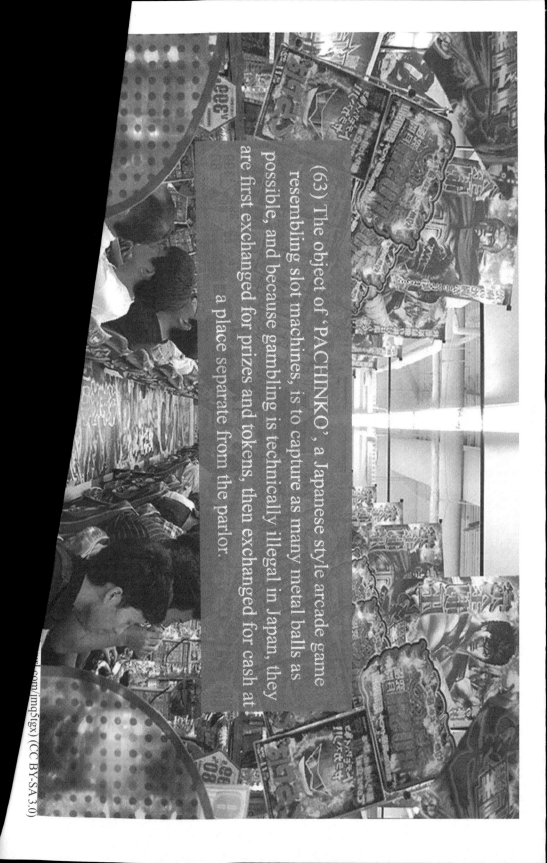

(63) The object of 'PACHINKO', a Japanese style arcade game resembling slot machines, is to capture as many metal balls as possible, and because gambling is technically illegal in Japan, they are first exchanged for prizes and tokens, then exchanged for cash at a place separate from the parlor.

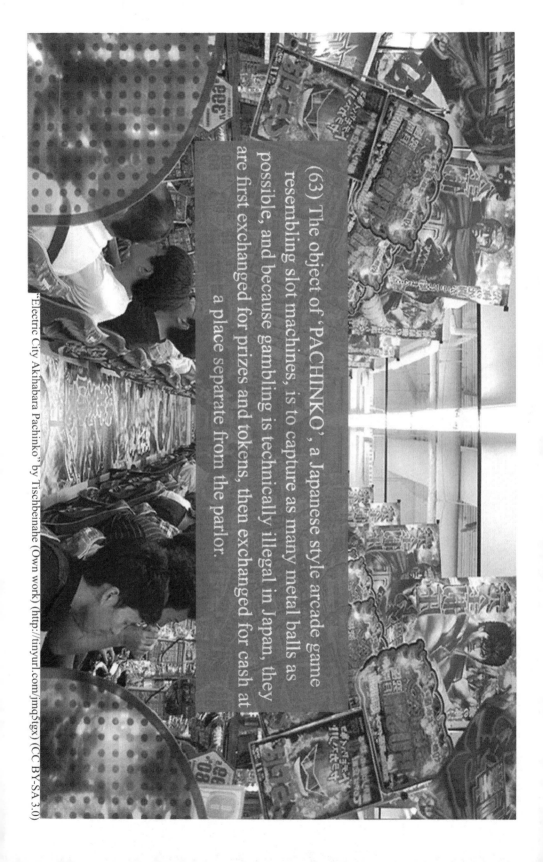

(63) The object of 'PACHINKO', a Japanese style arcade game resembling slot machines, is to capture as many metal balls as possible, and because gambling is technically illegal in Japan, they are first exchanged for prizes and tokens, then exchanged for cash at a place separate from the parlor.

(60) Japanese people use around 24 billion pairs of disposable chopsticks a year – this is equivalent to about 200 pairs per person, and it is the largest number of disposable chopsticks usage in the world. About 90% of them are imported from china, who produce more than 45 billion pairs a year.

(61) After breaking chopsticks apart, do not rub them together as it is usually done to remove wood splinters found on cheap chopsticks and it could send a signal that you think they are of low quality.

(62) Passing food from chopsticks to chopsticks is a big taboo as it resembles ceremoniously transfer-ring cremated bones to the urn.

1976

1976

(65) According to a survey done by Fuji Research Institute, Japanese people think instant noodles, a globally enjoyed food now, is their best invention of the 20th century.

(64) 'CUPNOODLES MUSEUM' is a 4-story museum in Yokohama, dedicated solely to cup noodles, and visitors can assemble their own personal cup noodles.

(66) When 'CHICKEN RAMEN', the world's first instant noodle invented by Momofuku Ando, made its debut in 1958, it was considered a luxury item.

SAKE

(67) Although 'SAKE' is considered "rice wine", it is more similar to beer as it is made through the brewing process – where the starch from rice is converted into sugars, and eventually, alcohol.

(68) October 1st is the official Nihonshu (Sake) day of Japan.

(69) When drinking Sake with others, pouring one's own drink is traditionally avoided – especially for the first drink in formal settings.

(70) Sake is served either chilled at room temperature or heated, depending on the drinker's preference, the quality of sake, and the season – typically, but not always, low-quality and old Sake is often served heated as doing it masks unpleasant flavors.

(71) Chances are pretty good that your zipper has 'YKK' engraved on it because YKK group of Japan manufactures half of all zippers in the world (7 billion).

(72) 'YKK' stands for 'YOSHIDA KOGYO KABUSHIKIGAISHA', which roughly translates to Yoshida manufacturing shareholding company

(73) On Christmas day, Kernel Sanders is as popular as Santa Claus – thanks to an extremely successful marketing campaign "Kentucky for Christmas" which first rolled out in 1974, Kentucky Fried Chicken has been the representative meal of Christmas – so popular that many people pre-order months in advance, or should you choose to wait in line, be ready to wait up to two hours.

(74) In Japan, there are over 200 Kit Kat flavors available, and among those are soy sauce, green tea, miso, grilled corn, lemon vinegar, custard pudding, sweet potato, and camembert cheese

(75) Kit Kats are an incredibly popular gift among students during entrance exam season because the name sounds similar to "KITTO KATSU" which means "surely win".

(76) 'Genius Energy,' 'Snow Squash', 'Fantastic Five', 'Hip Hop', and 'The Mystery Fruit' are some of the 70+ Fanta flavors available in Japan.

(77) Squid candy, cheese drink, curry lemon-ade, scallops and mayo flavored chips, ice cucumber pepsi, roasted baby crabs, eel soda, and beef tongue flavored ice cream are some of the unique snacks and drinks available in Japan.

(78) There is an 'ALL-BLACK BURGER' at Burger King in Japan. This unconventional burger featuring black buns, black cheese, black sauce, and fried eggplant, is a byproduct of a tactic developed by Burger King Japan's marketing team — with limited budget, they had to find a way to compete against the giant rival, mcdonald's, and the black burger was released to create buzz.

(79) Since the opening of its first store in 1971, Japan now (2015) has 2,975 McDonald's stores operating — the most in the world outside the U.S., and some of the notable menus only found in Japan include MEGA TERIYAKI BURGER, AmericaN FUNKY BBQ, LAS VEGAS BURGER, Sakura TERITAMA BURGER, CHEESE KATSU BURGER, AND WASABI MCNUGGET SAUCE.

(80) When McDonald's in Japan ran a special sale where they sold any-size French fries to just 150 Yen ($1.2 USD) per order, it started a viral frenzy known as "POTATO PARTY", among teens, where some went as far as ordering 60 large fries at once and devouring with friends — it ended only after the sale event was over.

(81) 'BASASHI' is a Japanese delicacy that consists of raw horse meat with onions and ginger—when raw horse meat is served alone, it is called 'SAKURANIKU (cherry blossom meat)' as its pink color resembles the flower.

(82) Scientists in Japan INVENTED A SPRAY FIRE ALARM FOR DEAF PEOPLE USING WASABI AS INGREDIENT, which effectively awoke a sleeping subject within 10 seconds – for which they won the ig nobel prize for chemistry in 2011.

(83) 'WALKMAN', Sony's mega-hit portable audio cassette player, was known as 'SOUNDABOUT' in the U.S., 'FREE-STYLE' in Sweden, 'STOWAWAY' in the U.K.

(84) Mirrors, ceramic wares, glasswares, knives, and scissors should be avoided as wedding gifts as THEY SYMBOLIZE BREAKING UP OR CUTTING (THE RELATIONSHIP).

(85) Instead of bullets, JAPANESE POLICE FIRE HARD-TO-REMOVE BRIGHT ORANGE-COLORED PAINTBALLS AT FLEEING VEHICLES, helping other police vehicles easily spot and identify them at a later time even if they get.

(86) In 1949, INDIA SENT 2 ELEPHANTS TO THE TOKYO ZOO TO CHEER THE SPIRITS OF THE DEFEATED JAPANESE EMPIRE.

(87) Despite the dangers of exposure to radiation, MORE THAN 200 ELDERLY JAPANESE PEOPLE VOLUNTEERED TO CLEAN UP AFTER THE DEVASTATING FUKUSHIMA NUCLEAR DISASTER so the younger generation wouldn't have to.

(88) JAPANESE GOLFERS PURCHASE INSURANCE TO PROTECT THEMSELVES IN CASE OF SINKING A HOLE-IN-ONE because it is customary for the lucky golfer to throw a lavish party for his/her golfing buddies, which can run as high as $10,000 USD.

(89) In Japan, a pet-loving country, a growing number of people choose pets in place of children, and THERE ARE MORE PETS THAN CHILDREN IN JAPAN – in 2009, there was a total of 23.2 Million cats and dogs, outnumbering children by 6 million.

(90) Unlike many countries around the globe, BLACK CATS ARE CONSIDERED A SYMBOL OF GOOD LUCK.

(91) 'MANEKI NEKO THE LUCKY CAT'

has different meanings depending on its color, paw position, and belongings

BLACK (safety)
GOLD (wealth and prosperity)
RED (protection from evil & illness)
PINK (love and romance)
GREEN (education)

RIGHT PAW (money and good fortune)
LEFT PAW (attracting customers)
BOTH (protection)

COIN (wealth and abundance)
BIB AND BELL (protection and abundance).

(92) 'KISHI STATION' was a financially underperforming location, but after it hired a cat named 'TAMA' to station manager, the station saw an increase in the number of passengers due to her ever growing popularity as an iconic mascot – her contribution was recog-nizedand she was promoted to "SUPER STATION MANAGER".

(93) Hello Kitty is not a human and not quite a cat either - she is actually a personification of a cat, described as a little English girl from outside London.

(94) Hello Kitty's full name is 'KITTY WHITE', and was originally known as "THE WHITE KITTEN WITH NO NAME".

(95) 'HANAMI', Japanese for 'flower viewing', entails picnicking under blooming 'SAKURA' (cherry blossoms) and was limited to only the elite of the imperial court.

(96) In Japan, Sakura symbolizes clouds because of their blooming en masse and used as a metaphor for the evanescent nature of life because of its beauty and quick fall.

(97) Pilots of 'Kamikaze', or suicide bombers during World War II, painted Sakura on the sides of their planes or even took branches of the trees with them before embarking on a suicide mission.

(98) 'Sakurayu', or salt-pickled blossoms in hot water, are drunk at festive event like wedding when green tea of green i

(99) Koi fish, or carp, have been bred for color in Japan since as early as the 1820's and there are over 22 varieties of them

(100) Chinatown in Yokohama is the largest in Asia and one of the largest in the world, boasting 150 years of history and 250 chinese-owned/themed shops and restaurants.

(101) 'CHANOYU', the Japanese tea ceremony of preparing and appreciating 'MATCHA' or powdered green tea, has its roots in Zen Buddhism and thus closely resembles its rituals.

(102) Contrary to popular belief, tea ceremonies were practiced almost entirely by men belonging to the upper class, up until the Meiji era (1868-1912).

(103) Around the 13th century, tea became a status symbol among the Samurai class, and there were tea-tasting parties that gave away extravagant prizes for those who guessed the best quality tea.

"The Tea Ceremony", Yōshū Chikanobu, March 3, 1895

(104) Japan is believed to have been inhabited since as early as 30,000 B.C.

(105) In 2014, Japan's population declined by 271,058 people, making it the largest drop and 6-year straight

(106) Sitting on top of four huge slabs of the earth's crust and along the Pacific Ring of Fire, Japan is one of the most volatile place on the globe - there are 1,500 earthquakes in Japan every year, and the great Kanto earth-quake of 1923 killed more than 100,000 people.

(107) Japan is the only place in the world where three plates (North American, Pacific, and Philippine) meet.

(108) Japan is an archipelago – a country composed of numerous islands with four main islands (Honshu, Hokkaido, Kyushu, and Shikoku) and their surrounding smaller islands – there are a total of 6,852 islands that make up this country.

(109) About 73% of the Japanese land is unsuitable for agricultural, industrial, and residential use.

(110) 15 Million years ago, Japan was attached to the eastern coast of the Eurasian continent, but the pulling of sub ducting plates caused separation.

(111) A large portion of the Jap-anese judicial system has been based on the civil law of Europe, especially that of Germany.

(112) The 'KANJI (adopted Chinese characters used in Japanese writing)' for Japan lit-erally means "ORIGIN OF THE SUN".

(113) The Japanese flag is officially called 'NISSHOKI (sun-mark flag)' and is more commonly known as 'HINOMARU (circle of the sun)'.

(114) The sun plays an important role in the Japanese mythology as well as religion, as the emperor is said to have been directly descended from 'AMATERASU', the female solar deity.

(115) There are over 50,000 people who are over the age of 100 – a dramatic increase from 153 people when the survey first started back in 1963.

(116) More than one-quarter (25.9%) Of the Japanese population are 65 years old or older, and there is a national holiday called "respect for the aged day", which honors the country's elders.

(117) Clearly reflecting its extremely low birthrate and the ever-growing population of the elderly citizens, adult diapers are sold more than baby diapers in Japan.

(118) When officials from Tokyo paid a visit to congratulate the oldest man in the city on his 111th birthday, they doubted their eyes – there were mummified skeletal remains on his bed, and he has been dead for 30 years while his family was taking in the pension money under his name.

(119) The 2011 tohoku earthquake was so massive that it in-creased the earth's rotation speed – according to NASA's jet propulsion laboratory in Pasadena, California, the redistribution of the planet's mass has accelerated the earth's spin, shortening the 24-hour day by 1.8 microseconds.

(120) When the earthquakes struck in 2011, there were ancient stone tablets warning about the disaster. These stones, some as old as 600 years, send a clear message— do not build homes below where they stand, and when tsunami hit the town, the waves stopped just 300 feet below the stones. It's a lesson from the past that history does repeat itself.

(121) Japan accounts for almost 15% of the fish caught in the world.

(122) The TSUKIJI MARKET is the biggest wholesale fish and seafood market in the world – handling more than 400 different types of seafood, from seaweed to caviar, and from tiny sardines to 300-kg tuna. More than 700,000 tons of seafood are handled every year, equivalent to 5.9 Billion USD.

(123) At Tsukiji fish market in 2013, a 222-kg blue fin tuna was sold for 1.8 million USD, and became the world's most expensive tuna ever sold – this is equal to 9,000 USD per kilogram of tuna.

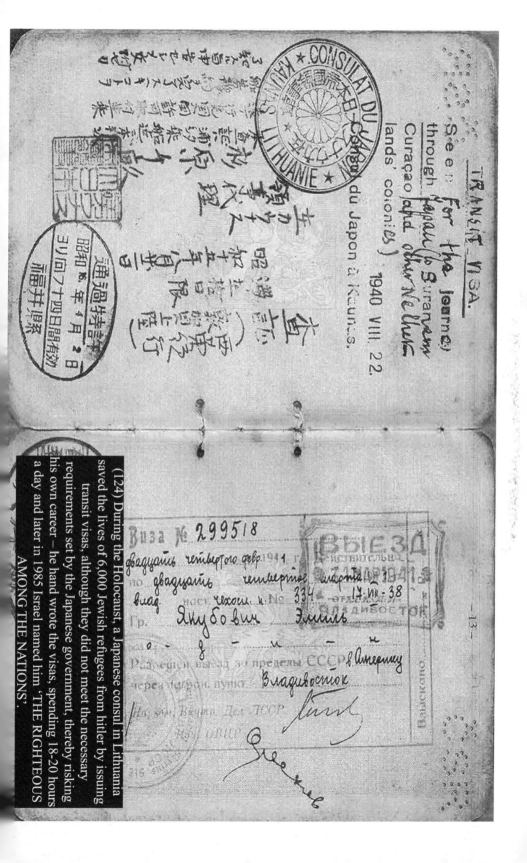

TRANSIT VISA.

Seen For the journey
through Japan (to Suranam
Curaçao and other Nether
lands' colonies)
1940 VIII. 22.

(Consul du Japon à Kaun.s)

Виза № 299518

двадцать четвертого февр 1941 г.
по двадцать четвертое марта 1941 г.
влад. ности чехосл. к № 334 — 17. VII - 38

Гр. Якубович Эмиль

Разрешен выезд за пределы СССР в Америку

через границ. пункт Владивосток

На зам. Нач. Деп. ГСССР
Нач. ОВИР

– 13 –

(124) During the Holocaust, a Japanese consul in Lithuania saved the lives of 6,000 Jewish refugees from hitler by issuing transit visas, although they did not meet the necessary requirements set by the Japanese government, thereby risking his own career — he hand wrote the visas, spending 18-20 hours a day and later in 1985 Israel named him 'THE RIGHTEOUS AMONG THE NATIONS'.

(125) The imperial regalia of Japan, also known as the 'THREE SACRED TREASURES OF Japan', consist of the sword, the mirror, and the jewel, each representing valor, wisdom, and benevolence – they are extremely sacred to the point that their locations have not been publically confirmed, but only the emperor and a few priests at the shrine get a chance to see during the enthronement ceremony.

(126) Made of pure aluminum, a 1 Yen coin weighs just 1 gram, and if placed carefully on the surface of still water, it won't break surface tension and float on it.

(127) One of the most bizarre creatures of Japanese folklore is 'ASHIRAI YASHIKI' – a mud-and-blood-covered giant foot that smashes its way into the homes of humans and demands them to wash it.

Ashiaraiyashiki from the Honjo-nana-fushigi, circa 1886

"Kawauso" by Toriyama Sekien

(128) In Japanese
folklore, otters are portrayed as evil
creatures where they fool and
even kill people by shapeshifting into
beautiful women or children wearing
checker-patterned clothing.

(129) According to a Japanese folklore, there is a rabbit living on the moon, portrayed as constantly pounding the ingredients to make 'MOCHI (rice cake)'.

(130) 'MOCHI', chewy Japanese rice cake made with glutinous rice, is enjoyed as a snack and a dessert, especially during festive times like the New Year's Day – but more than 100 people are sent to the hospital every year from choking on it.

(131) 'WASHOKU', the traditional Japanese cuisine, is an intangible cultural heritage asset designated by UNESCO.

(132) As of 2013, restaurant KITCHO in Kyoto is the most expensive restaurant in the world, averaging $600 USD per person – it features the essence of KAISEKI, a ceremonious multi-course affairs originated with Japanese tea ceremonies.

(133) 'SHOKADO BENTO', the traditional black-lacquered Japanese lunchbox, inspired the design of IBM's Thinkpad laptops.

(134) When eating certain foods such as Ramen noodle soup, slurping is perfectly acceptable and is even considered a compliment, but blowing your nose in public, especially at a restaurant, is frowned upon.

(135) The SAPPORO SNOW FESTIVAL, one of Japan's largest and most unique winter events, began in 1950 when high school students built small snow statues, which later followed in 1955 by the Japanese Self-Defense Forces that joined and built the first massive snow sculptures.

(136) During 'HADAKA FESTIVAL', thousands of Japanese men, covering only their privates with loincloths, struggle with one another to catch a pair of lucky sacred sticks. The priest throws them into the crowd from a window 4 meters up, and the one who catches and thrusts them upright in a wooden box full of rice is honored and blessed with a year of happiness.

(137) 'KANAMARA MATSURI', or "FESTIVAL OF THE STEEL PHALLUS", is a Shinto festival held each spring at the Kanayama shrine in Kawasaki, where they venerate the male penis. This is based on the legend that a blacksmith made an iron penis that broke the teeth of a demon that hid inside of the vagina of a young woman and castrated 2 young men on their wedding nights.

(138) 'ISE JINGU GRAND SHRINE' of Mie prefecture is torn down and rebuilt every 20 years in order to preserve the original architect's design against eroding effects of time — a tradition that has been kept alive for the past 1,300 years.

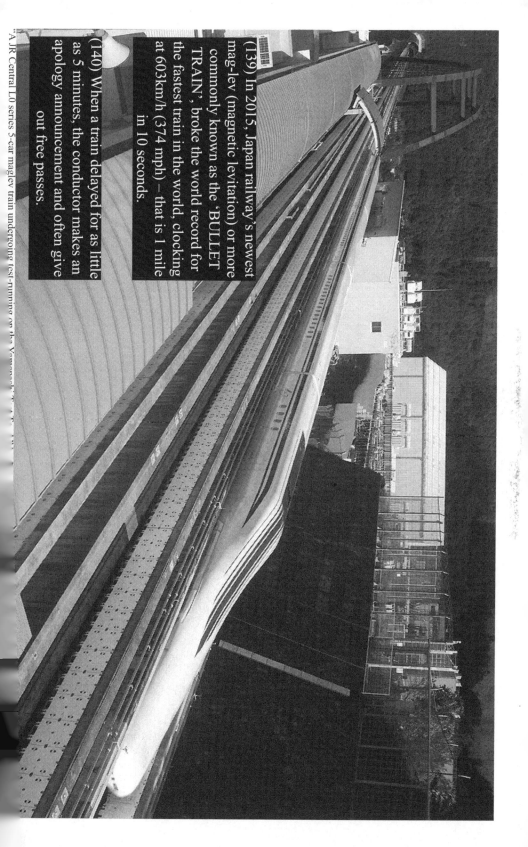

(139) In 2015, Japan railway's newest mag-lev (magnetic levitation) or more commonly known as the 'BULLET TRAIN', broke the world record for the fastest train in the world, clocking at 603km/h (374 mph) – that is 1 mile in 10 seconds.

(140) When a train delayed for as little as 5 minutes, the conductor makes an apology announcement and often give out free passes.

(141) Shinjuku station is the busiest station in the world. On average, it transports about 3,640,000 passengers per day.

(142) Every time the light changes at Shibuya crossing, as many as 2,500 pedestrians cross the intersection at the same time – this is equivalent to 1 million people a day.

(143) Composed of only three lines, 'HAIKU' is the shortest form of poetry in the world – to make it even more sophisticated, first line has to be expressed in 5 syllables, middle line in 7 syllables, and final line in 5 syllables.

"A litrle cuckoo across a hydrangea(Haiga)" by Yosa Buson

(144) 'THE TALE OF GENJI', a 54-chapter-long Japanese literature masterpiece written in the early 11th century by the Japanese noblewoman and lady-in-waiting, Murasaki Shikibu, is acknowledged to be the world's first novel.

Ilustration of the The Tale of Genji, ch.5–Wakamurasaki, traditionally credited to Tosa Mitsuoki (1617–1691), part of the Burke Albums, property of Mary Griggs Burke

(145) 'HOSHI RYOKAN (Japanese traditional inn)' was founded in 718, and has been in business for nearly 13 centuries, by the same family for 46 generations.

(147) Japanese houses have raised floors at 'GENKAN', the entryway, to indicate when to take off the shoes – they usually put on slippers indoors.

(146) Japanese people have a tendency to separate areas into 'clean' and 'unclean', and try to minimize the contact between the two. So much so that they keep separate pairs of 'TOILET SLIPPERS' which they put on upon entering the bathroom.

(148) With blocks roughly measuring at 2 x 1 x 1.25 Meters (6'7" x 3'3" x 4'1") each, Japan's 'CAPSULE HOTEL' is the tiniest hotel in the world. Since its first debut in the Umeda district of Osaka in 1979, it's been an ideal solution especially for people who are too drunk to return home safely or too embarrassed to face their spouses.

(149) Baseball, or 'YAKYU' in Japanese, was first introduced in 1872 by an American English professor, Horace Wilson, and became the most popular sport ever since.

(150) The first Japanese baseball team was established in 1878, with the name 'SHIMBASHI ATHLETIC CLUB'.

(151) Some of the notable differences of Japanese baseball from American baseball are: Japanese balls have more tighter winding around the core, the strike zone tends to be narrower inside than away from the batter, and tie games are allowed.

(152) Mario of the mega hit video game series 'SUPER MARIO BROTHERS', was originally a carpenter, not a plumber.

(153) Mario has been called 'THE MOST RECOGNIZABLE CHARACTER' in the gaming industry, even surpassing Mickey Mouse in a national survey done in the 1990's.

(154) Roughly translated, 'NINTENDO' means "LEAVE LUCK TO HEAVEN" in Japanese.

(155) As of 2013, Japan has 20% of the world's industrial robots (300,000 of 1.3 Million).

(156) The term 'KARAOKE' means "EMPTY ORCHESTRA".

(157) Besides enjoying green tea, Japanese people drink about 350 cups of coffee annually – almost 1 cup of coffee everyday, and Japan imports about 80% of coffee produced in Jamaica.

(158) The Japanese movie 'THE HIDDEN FORTRESS' by Kurosawa Akira, is what inspired 'STAR WARS EPISODE IV: A NEW HOPE', with Matasichi and Tahei serving as models for R2-D2 and C-3P0.

(159) World War II ended but JAPAN AND RUSSIA ARE STILL AT WAR – because of an ongoing territorial dispute over Kuril Islands (known as the Northern Territories in Japan) dating back to the end of World War II, they still haven't signed a peace treaty. Japan has been demanding the return of the islands taken by the Soviet Union in the final phases of the war.

(160) AT RESTAURANT 'MR. KANSO', EVERYTHING COMES IN A CAN – diners can choose from a variety of 300 canned foods from all across the world. The whole browsing experience and trying out new flavors are what keeps the business going. Since its opening in 2002, it continues to grow with more than 40 outlets across Japan.

161) In 1997, after watching a Pokémon episode "DENNO SENSHI ÐRYGON", 685 kids were rushed to the hospital - it featured a scene here Pikachu uses an electric shock, making tv screen flash red and blue rapidly, possibly causing epileptic seizures.

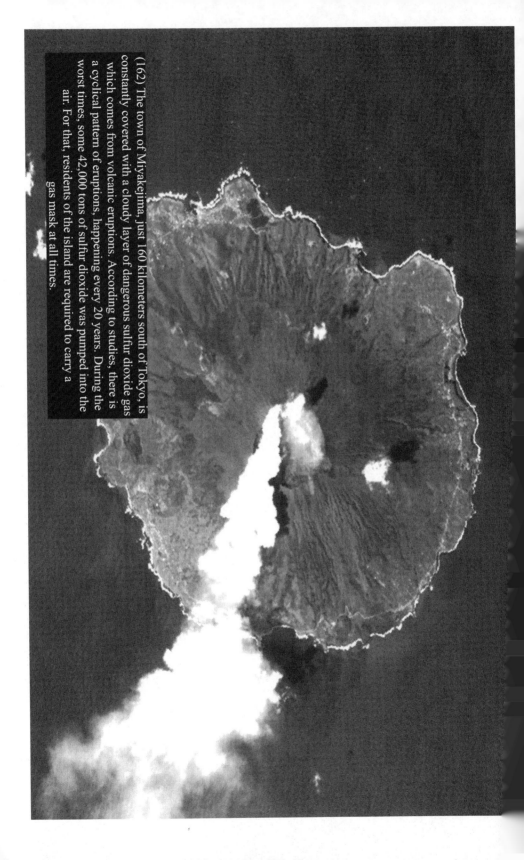

(162) The town of Miyakejima, just 160 kilometers south of Tokyo, is constantly covered with a cloudy layer of dangerous sulfur dioxide gas which comes from volcanic eruptions. According to studies, there is a cyclical pattern of eruptions, happening every 20 years. During the worst times, some 42,000 tons of sulfur dioxide was pumped into the air. For that, residents of the island are required to carry a gas mask at all times.

(163) There is an island dominated by rabbits and there are two theories surrounding their proliferation. First theory is that during World War II, Japanese army secretly produced poisonous gas on 'Okunoshima' island, where they brought a colony of rabbits to test the effectiveness of the gas, and the surviving rabbits were released at the end of the war. Another theory argues they are the descendents of the 8 rabbits brought to the island by school children in 1971.

A poster used in Japan to attract immigrants to Brazil. It reads: "Let's go to South America (Brazil highlighted) with families."

(164) The largest Japanese community outside Japan is found in Brazil, where there are between 1.4 and 1.5 Million of them. The first wave of immigration was fueled by the end of feudalism which resulted in great poverty in the rural population. For this reason, many chose Brazil where there were work opportunities, especially on coffee plants.

(165) Bathing is an important element of the Japanese lifestyle, but it is only for relaxing and not cleansing – body must be cleaned and scrubbed before entering the bathtub.

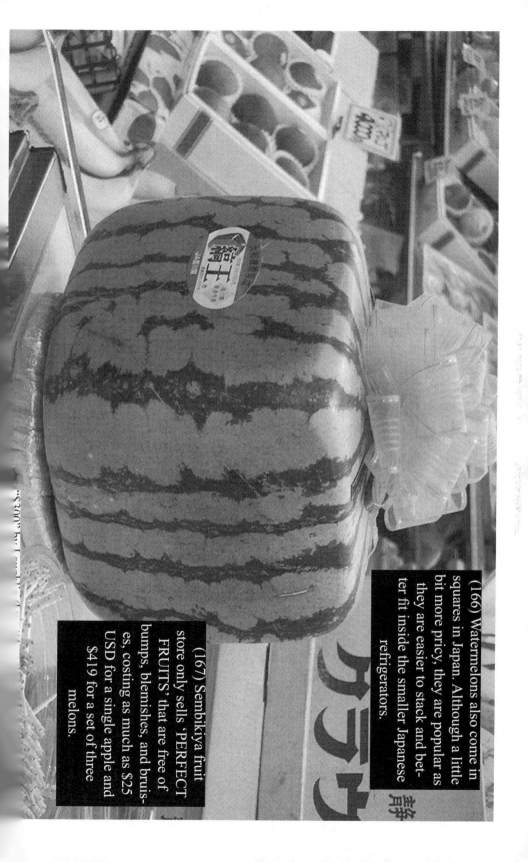

(166) Watermelons also come in squares in Japan. Although a little bit more pricy, they are popular as they are easier to stack and better fit inside the smaller Japanese refrigerators.

(167) Sembikiya fruit store only sells 'PERFECT FRUITS' that are free of bumps, blemishes, and bruises, costing as much as $25 USD for a single apple and $419 for a set of three melons.

(168) Narita International Airport, Kansai International Airport, and Chubu Centrair International Airport are the largest international gateways.

(169) As the name suggests, the Japanese military, known as 'SELF-DEFENSE FORCE',

HAS NEVER FIRED SHOTS OUTSIDE JAPAN

this is because after World War II, Japan and the U.S. Signed the treaty of mutual cooperation and security, which limited the Japanese military forces to dealing with internal threats and natural disasters while having the U.S. Forces stationed in Japan deal with external aggressions against Japan.

(170) Japan has over 100 volcanoes that are still active at this moment, and that makes up 10% of the world's active volcanoes.

(172) The volcanic crater of Mt. Mihara is where the Japanese government imprisoned Godzilla – in the following sequel, Godzilla was released when bombs placed on Mt. Mihara went off.

(171) In 1933, a Japanese school girl committed suicide by throwing herself into a volcanic crater of Mt. Mihara and this started a bizarre trend where more than 1,000 people committed suicide by jumping into a volcanic crater. This horrible trend faded away only after the local government built a fence around the area.

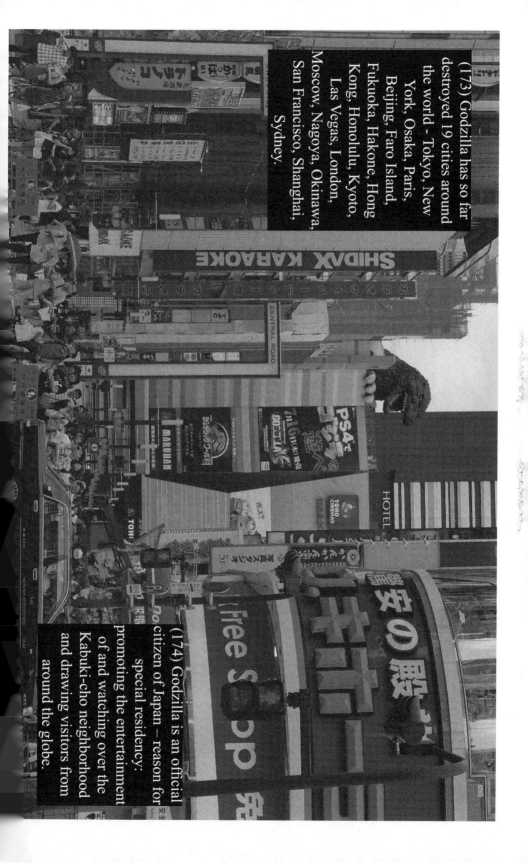

(173) Godzilla has so far destroyed 19 cities around the world - Tokyo, New York, Osaka, Paris, Beijing, Faro Island, Fukuoka, Hakone, Hong Kong, Honolulu, Kyoto, Las Vegas, London, Moscow, Nagoya, Okinawa, San Francisco, Shanghai, Sydney.

(174) Godzilla is an official citizen of Japan — reason for special residency: promoting the entertainment of and watching over the Kabuki-cho neighborhood and drawing visitors from around the globe.

空手

(175) According to world Karate foundation, there are 100 million people practicing Karate.

(177) UFC fighters Chuck Liddell, Frank Mir, Stephen Thompson, Lyoto Machida, John Makdessi, Bas Rutten, and Georges St. Pierre practice Karate.

(176) The Soviet Union government banned Karate twice, in 1973 and 1984, endorsing only the soviet martial art of Sambo.

(178) Dancing after midnight used to be illegal until recently because during World War II, dancehalls were commonly used as a hotbed for prostitution – an archaic law that has been largely overlooked has finally been lifted.

Kongō Yoshie, the 38th master carpenter of Kongō Gumi.

(179) Established in 578 A.D.,
'KONGO GUMI', a successful Japanese company specializing in the construction of spectacular Buddhist temples, lasted for more than 1,400 years – it was the world's oldest continuously operating family business but failed to survive through the hard times of Japan's economic downturn. It was purchased by the Takamatsu Construction Group in 2006.

TOKYO DOME

(180) In 1998, all of the 200,000 tickets for Mariah Carey's concert at the Tokyo Dome was sold out just under an hour — beating her own record of selling 150,000 tickets in less than 3 hours 2 years prior to that.

(181) The longest concert at the Tokyo Dome was by Guns N' Roses in 2009, which ran for 3 hours and 37 minutes non-stop. The set list consisted of 42 songs.

(182) Tokyo's urban legend has it that if a couple takes a boat ride on the pond at INOKASHIRA PARK, they can break up prematurely because doing it makes BENZAITEN (the guardian of the pond) jealous.

aiten Surrounded by the Goddesses Kariteimo and Kenrōchijin and Two Divine Generals, back wall of a Kichijōten iture shrine, c. 1212, polychrome wood, 103.5 x 62.7 cm., University Art Museum, Tokyo University of the Arts

(183) First introduced in 1888, there are 5.52 million vending machines in Japan, with annual sales reaching almost 6.95 trillion Yen (58 billion USD) – the highest penetration rate in ratio to land in the world.

(184) Rice, batteries, crepes, flowers, pantyhose, eggs, glasses, cold draft beer, books, french fries, hot dogs, fried chicken, liquor, umbrellas, milk, ice cubes, sushi, cup noodles, and cars are sold through Japanese vending machines.

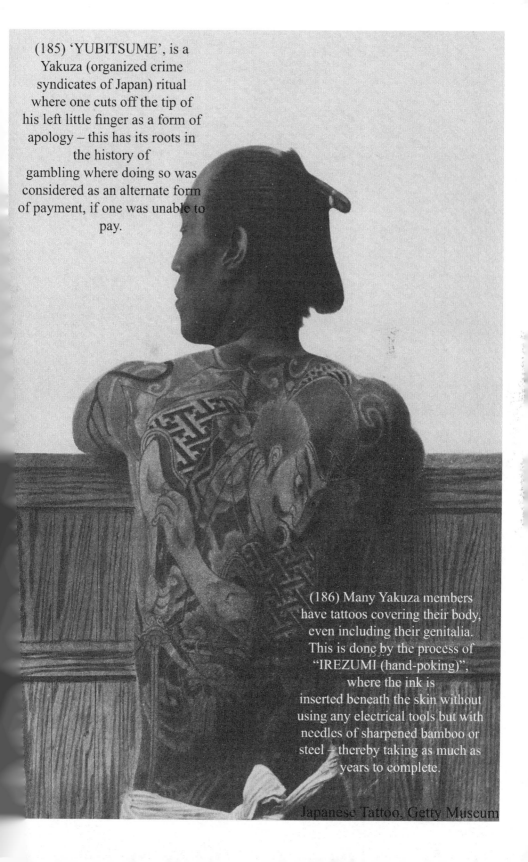

(185) 'YUBITSUME', is a Yakuza (organized crime syndicates of Japan) ritual where one cuts off the tip of his left little finger as a form of apology – this has its roots in the history of gambling where doing so was considered as an alternate form of payment, if one was unable to pay.

(186) Many Yakuza members have tattoos covering their body, even including their genitalia. This is done by the process of "IREZUMI (hand-poking)", where the ink is inserted beneath the skin without using any electrical tools but with needles of sharpened bamboo or steel – thereby taking as much as years to complete.

Japanese Tattoo, Getty Museum

187) GEISHA, traditional Japanese female entertainers who are highly skilled at various performing arts, couldn't get married until retired, as they are expected to be single women.

(188) 'JUNIHO-TE', meaning "twelve-layer robe" in Japanese, is an extremely elegant and highly complex Kimono only worn by court ladies, and the total of the layers could add up to 20kg (44lbs).

(189) Japanese women considered BLACK TEETH A THING OF BEAUTY

Woodblock print by Tsukioka Yoshitoshi, series 'Twenty-Four Hours at Shinbashi and Yanagibashi', print # 13 (1 p.m.), 1880

so 'OHAGURO', a custom of blackening teeth with dye, was popular until the late 1800's. On the bright side, however, it helped prevent tooth decay.

(190) Known for its succulence and taste, Japanese KOBE

COWS ARE RAISED WITH TENDER LOVING CARE

some owners would go as far as brushing them with Sake to make their hair silky, giving daily massages to relieve stress, and feeding beer to stimulate appetite.

(191) With 9 distilleries, Japan is the third largest producer of whisky blends behind scotland and the U.S., But before Ireland, contributing to 5% of all world-wide whisky sales.

(192) The most popular way to enjoy whisky in Japan is 'Highball', made by mixing whisky, ice cubes, and soda water. Popular because casual drinkers prefer to enjoy the flavor of whisky that is not too intense to be had with a meal.

(193) There is a building that has a highway going right through it – the Hanshin Expressway occupies floors 5,6,7 of the Gate Tower Building in Osaka. This is a result of a compromise between the landowner who wanted to re-develop the building and the government who had already planned the expressway. It took 5 years of negotiations to finally come up with this solution.

(194) In the basement levels of More's department store in Kawasaki, there is a record-holding escalator which stands at 83.4Cm (32.8 Inches) tall with 5 steps. It takes just 4.6 Seconds to complete a one way trip on the world's shortest escalator.

(195) At 'MANGA KISSA', or manga café, customers can read manga at an hourly rate or even overnight – there is even a whole demographic of kids literally living there because it only costs $10 - $20 USD per night.

(196) More than 500 categories of manga are released each month, and Japanese people use more paper for comics than for toilet paper.

(197) 'One piece', the best selling manga of all time, has sold more than 320 million copies worldwide.

(198) With Japan being the biggest animation producing country in the world (60% of the world's total), there are over 130 voice acting schools in Japan, where many choose to become the voices of an animation characters.

(199) 'HACHIKO', a loyal Akita dog, devotedly waited for the return of his deceased owner for more than 9 years in front of Tokyo's Shibuya station, where Hachiko used to greet the owner returning from work.

(200) In 2015, the faculty of Agriculture of the University of Tokyo erected a bronze statue, depicting the owner returning to meet Hachiko.

緑の風公園

上野英三郎博士とハチ公

(201) Japanese author Yume-Hotaru wrote the world's first novel, 'Maho-No-Airando (magic island)', **ENTIRELY ON A CELL PHONE.**

(202) At 'SOINEYA', or 'cuddle café', **CUSTOMERS PAY TO TAKE A CUDDLE NAP IN THE ARMS (OR ON THE LAP) OF A GIRL.**

(203) The Japanese way of communication heavily incorporates subtleness and implication, evidenced by the fact that **THERE ARE AT LEAST 20 WAYS TO SAY SORRY IN JAPANESE.**

(204) In Japan, **GREEN TRAFFIC LIGHT ARE DESCRIBED AS "BLUE LIGHTS"**, because the Japanese Kanji (adopted chinese characters) used is derived from 'ao', which covers the spectrum of both green and blue.

(205) Bowing is extremely important in Japanese etiquette – **CHILDREN ARE TAUGHT HOW TO BOW** from a very young age and companies often provide training to their employees on proper bowing.

(206) **WRITING SOMEONE'S NAME IN RED INK** should be avoided as doing so is considered as wishing that person to die – and red is also used for the names written on grave markers.

(207) In Japan, **BLOOD TYPE DEFINES WHO YOU ARE** – employers often ask blood types during interview, children at some schools are split up according to their blood type, the national softball team have a customized training program to fit each player's blood type, and some companies gave work assignments according to the employees' blood type.

(208) Many Japanese women would keep flushing the toilet as they feel embarrassed of being heard during urination – so a company **INVENTED A DEVICE THAT EFFECTIVELY MASKS THE SOUND BY PRODUCING THE FLUSHING SOUND** at the touch of a button.

(209) During feudal Japan (12th – 19th century), **MERCHANTS WERE THE LOWEST CLASS BECAUSE THEY WERE CONSIDERED AS 'PARASITES'** who profited from the labor of peasants and artisans.

(210) 165 People **SURVIVED BOTH NUCLEAR BOMBINGS OF HIROSHIMA AND NAGASAKI** during World War II.

(211) **THERE ARE 4 WRITING SYSTEMS IN JAPAN**, KANJI (adopted chinese characters), HIRAGANA (for native Japanese words and grammar), KATAKANA (foreign words, loan words, scientific names, emphasis), and ROMAJI (romanized spelling to translate Japanese).

(212) Originally named after the founder's name, Kiichiro Toyoda, **ITS NAME BECOMES 'TOYOTA' AS IT SOUNDED MORE CLEAR AND CONSISTED EIGHT BRUSH STROKES WHEN WRITTEN IN JAPANESE, WHICH IS CONSIDERED LUCKY.**

(213) 'NIHONZARU', or Japanese macaques (snow monkeys), are native to Japan and are famous for their winter visits to enjoy bathing in hot springs and rolling snowballs for fun.

(214) At midnight on 'SHOGATSU (New Year's Eve)', Buddhist temples all over Japan toll their bells for a total of 108 times because it symbolizes the 108 human sins in Buddhist belief, as well as to get rid of the 108 worldly desires.

(215) Buddhist monks of Yamagata in the northern part of Japan practiced 'SOKUSHINBUTSU', a self-mummification process where they exercise rigorously, drink poisonous tea, and fast to rid all intestinal fat and bacteria – the mummified bodies are often found inside stupas along with relics.

(216) 'KARESANSUI', or Japanese rock gardens, use white sand which is carefully raked to symbolize water.

(217) The Japanese imperial family has been maintaining its unbroken lineage for the past 2,000 years, longest in human history.

"The Meiji Emperor of Japan and the imperial family..."

(218) KABUKI, the traditional Japanese theatre, was originally performed by both male and female actors, but today it is only played by male actors, and male actors also play the role of female characters.

(219) 'KUROKO' are stagehands who set and remove stage props, and they are dressed all in black and are considered invisible by the audience and the actors.

Woodblock print by Utagawa Kuniyoshi of actor Nakamura Shikan II as Ohatsu in the Kabuki play Sakura doki onne gyoretsu, showing three Kuroko, 3rd month of 1832

(220) At the height of World War II, Kyoto, full of Japan's many cultural assets, was on the verge of getting nuclear-bombed – but Henry L. Stimson, the secretary of war at the time asked it to be removed from the list because he had known and admired Kyoto ever since his honeymoon several decades earlier.

(221) Although popular in Chinese restaurants, fortune cookies have its roots in the Kyoto tradition of 'OMIKUJI', where random fortunes were written on strips of paper at Shinto shrines and Buddhist temples.

SOURCES & REFERENCES

(1) Norway's Introduction of Salmon Sushi to Japan. (2011, August 4). Retrieved December 28, 2015, from http://www.nortrade.com/sectors/articles/norways-introduction-of-salmon-sushi-to-japan/

(2) Sushi. (n.d.). Retrieved December 30, 2015, from https://en.wikipedia.org/wiki/Sushi

(3) California roll. (n.d.). Retrieved December 30, 2015, from https://en.wikipedia.org/wiki/California_roll

(4) Hill, Amelia October, 8, 2007. Chopsticks at dawn for a sushi showdown. London: The Guardian. Retrieved January 12, 2016.

(5) (8) (10) (11) (12) (16) Sushi. (n.d.). Retrieved December 30, 2015, from https://en.wikipedia.org/wiki/Sushi

(6) Honey, Kim (March 18, 2009). Are you sushi savvy?. Toronto Star. Retrieved 2009-11-09.

(7) Harness, J. (2012, September 14). 15 of the world's most expensive foods. Mental Floss. Retrieved January 4, 2016, from http://mentalfloss.com/article/12531/15-world's-most-expensive-foods

(8) Sushi. (n.d.). Retrieved December 30, 2015, from https://en.wikipedia.org/wiki/Sushi

(9) Zschock, Day. The Little Black Book of Sushi: The Essential Guide to the World of Sushi. Page 14-15. 2005. ISBN 1-59359-961-7.

(10) Sushi. (n.d.). Retrieved December 30, 2015, from https://en.wikipedia.org/wiki/Sushi

(11) Sushi. (n.d.). Retrieved December 30, 2015, from https://en.wikipedia.org/wiki/Sushi

(12) Sushi. (n.d.). Retrieved December 30, 2015, from https://en.wikipedia.org/wiki/Sushi

(13) Gordenker, Alice (2008-01-15). "Bento grass". The Japan Times Online. ISSN 0447-5763. Retrieved September 9, 2015.

(14) Gordenker, Alice (2008-01-15). "Bento grass". The Japan Times Online. ISSN 0447-5763. Retrieved September 9, 2015.

(15) Japanese cutlery. (n.d.). Retrieved December 30, 2015, from https://en.wikipedia.org/wiki/Japanese_cutlery

(16) Sushi. (n.d.). Retrieved December 30, 2015, from https://en.wikipedia.org/wiki/Sushi

(17) Buerk, R. (2012, May 18). Fugu: The fish more poisonous than cyanide. BBC. Retrieved January 6, 2016, from http://www.bbc.com/news/magazine-18065372

(18) Buerk, R. (2012, May 18). Fugu: The fish more poisonous than cyanide. BBC. Retrieved January 6, 2016, from http://www.bbc.com/news/magazine-18065372

(19) MT. Fuji. (n.d.). Retrieved December 30, 2015, from https://en.wikipedia.org/wiki/MT._Fuji

(20) MT. Fuji. (n.d.). Retrieved December 30, 2015, from https://en.wikipedia.org/wiki/MT._Fuji

(21) MT. Fuji. (n.d.). Retrieved December 30, 2015, from https://en.wikipedia.org/wiki/MT._Fuji

(22) Launching Infiniti. Lippincott.

(23) Alcock, Rutherford (1863). The Capital of the Tycoon: A Narrative of Three Years Residence in Japan I. London: Longman, Green, Longman, Roberts & Green.

(24) MT. Fuji. (n.d.). Retrieved December 30, 2015, from https://en.wikipedia.org/wiki/MT._Fuji

(25) Cortazzi, Hugh et al. Britain and Japan, 1859-1991, pp. 99-100.

(26) MT. Fuji. (n.d.). Retrieved December 30, 2015, from https://en.wikipedia.org/wiki/MT._Fuji

(27) Samurai. (n.d.). Retrieved December 30, 2015, from https://en.wikipedia.org/wiki/Samurai

(28) Samurai. (n.d.). Retrieved December 30, 2015, from https://en.wikipedia.org/wiki/Samurai

(29) Samurai. (n.d.). Retrieved December 30, 2015, from https://en.wikipedia.org/wiki/Samurai

(30) Mehrotra, Morck, Shim, Wiwattanakantang. Adoptive Expectations:Rising Sons in Japanese Family Firms.

(31) Awamura, Ryoichi (December 11, 2003). Spain's Japon clan has reunion to trace its 17th century roots. The Japan Times. Retrieved October 14, 2015.

(32) Samurai. (n.d.). Retrieved December 30, 2015, from https://en.wikipedia.org/wiki/Samurai

(33) Turnbull, Stephen (2003), Ninja AD 1460–1650, p. 12. Osprey Publishing, ISBN 978-1-84176-525-9

(34) Turnbull, Stephen (2003), Ninja AD 1460–1650, p. 12. Osprey Publishing, ISBN 978-1-84176-525-9

(35) Draeger, Donn F.; Smith, Robert W. (1981), Comprehensive Asian fighting arts, Kodansha, ISBN 978-0-87011-436-6, p. 125.

(36) Draeger, Donn F.; Smith, Robert W. (1981), Comprehensive Asian fighting arts, Kodansha, ISBN 978-0-87011-436-6, p. 125.

(37) Ninja. (n.d.). Retrieved December 30, 2015, from https://en.wikipedia.org/wiki/Ninja

(38) Ninja. (n.d.). Retrieved December 30, 2015, from https://en.wikipedia.org/wiki/Ninja

(39) Willey, N. (November 11, 2015). 10 Revealing facts about the Katana. Listverse. Retrieved January 5, 2016, from http://listverse.com/2015/11/12/10-

(40) Willey, N. (November 11, 2015). 10 Revealing facts about the Katana. Listverse. Retrieved January 5, 2016, from http://listverse.com/2015/11/12/10-revealing-facts-about-the-katana/

(41) Reif, R. (April 1, 1992). Record Prices at Christie's For Japanese Swords. The New York Times. Retrieved January 5, 2016.

(42) Shinken. (n.d.). Retrieved May 19, 2015, from https://en.wikipedia.org/wiki/Shinken

(43) Shigeru Takayama. Encyclopedia of Shinto:Sumo. http://eos.kokugakuin.ac.jp. Retrieved January 13, 2016.

(44) 11 Things You Might Not Know About Sumo. (2013, December 14). Japan Talk. Retrieved January 6, 2016, from http://www.japan-talk.com/jt/new/11-things-you-might-not-know-about-Sumo

(45) 11 Things You Might Not Know About Sumo. (2013, December 14). Japan Talk. Retrieved January 6, 2016, from http://www.japan-talk.com/jt/new/11-things-you-might-not-know-about-Sumo

(46) Sumo. (n.d.). Retrieved December 30, 2015, from https://en.wikipedia.org/wiki/Sumo

(47) Yes, it's the 'Crying Sumo' contest: Japanese wrestlers compete to see who can make a baby bawl. (2010, April 26). Dailymail. Retrieved December 28, 2015, from http://www.dailymail.co.uk/news/article-1268867/The-crying-sumo-contest-Japanese-wrestlers-compete-make-baby-first.html

(48) Greater Tokyo area. (n.d.). Retrieved December 13, 2015, from https://en.wikipedia.org/wiki/Greater_Tokyo_Area

(49) Dwyer, C. (2015, October 14). What makes Tokyo the world's greatest food city? CNN. Retrieved January 12, 2016, from http://edition.cnn.com/2015/10/12/foodanddrink/tokyo-world-greatest-food-city/

(50) Nussbaum, Louis-Frédéric. (2005). "Tōkyō" in Japan Encyclopedia, pp. 981–982, p. 981, at Google Books; "Kantō" in p. 479, p. 479, at Google Books

(51) http://safecities.economist.com/infographics/safe-cities-index-infographic/

(52) Hewitt, Kenneth (1983). "Place Annihilation: Area Bombing and the Fate of Urban Places". Annals of the Association of American Geographers 73 (2): 257–284. doi:10.1111/j.1467-8306.1983.tb01412.x.

(53) List of amusement park rankings. (n.d.). Retrieved December 30, 2015, from https://en.wikipedia.org/wiki/List_of_amusement_park_rankings

(54) Global 500 Our annual ranking of the world's largest corporationns. CNNMoney.com. Retrieved December 11, 2015

(55) Tokyo. (n.d.). Retrieved December 30, 2015, from https://en.wikipedia.org/wiki/Tokyo

(56) Tokyo. (n.d.). Retrieved December 30, 2015, from https://en.wikipedia.org/wiki/Tokyo

(57) Tokyo. (n.d.). Retrieved December 30, 2015, from https://en.wikipedia.org/wiki/Tokyo

(58) Tokyo. (n.d.). Retrieved December 30, 2015, from https://en.wikipedia.org/wiki/Tokyo

(59) Japan Finishes World's Tallest Communications Tower. Council on Tall Buildings and Urban Habitat. March 1, 2012. Retrieved Jan 1, 2016.

(60) Rising Chinese chopstick prices help Japan firm". Asia Times Online. Asia Times. Retrieved October 11, 2015.

(61) Emiko. (2009, November 11). 10 Golden rules for Japanese chopstick manners. Japan Talk. Retrieved January 3, 2016, from http://www.japan-talk.com/jt/new/10-golden-rules-for-japanese-chopstick-manners

(62) Emiko. (2009, November 11). 10 Golden rules for Japanese chopstick manners. Japan Talk. Retrieved January 3, 2016, from http://www.japan-talk.com/jt/new/10-golden-rules-for-japanese-chopstick-manners

(63) Pachinko. (n.d.). Retrieved December 30, 2015, from https://en.wikipedia.org/wiki/Pachinko

(64) Momofuku Ando Instant Ramen Museum. (n.d.). Retrieved December 30, 2015, from https://en.wikipedia.org/wiki/Momofuku_Ando_Instant_Ramen_Museum

(65) Japan votes noodle the tops. (2000, December 12). BBC. Retrieved January 9, 2016, from http://news.bbc.co.uk/2/hi/asia-pacific/1067506.stm

(66) About us. (n.d.). Nissin Foods. Retrieved January 9, 2016, from https://www.nissinfoods.com/about.php

(67) Sake. (n.d.). Retrieved December 30, 2015, from https://en.wikipedia.org/wiki/Sake

(68) Sake Service Institute. October 1st becomes the official day of nihonshu (in Japanese). Retrieved December 12, 2015.

(69) Sake. (n.d.). Retrieved December 30, 2015, from https://en.wikipedia.org/wiki/Sake

(70) Sake. (n.d.). Retrieved December 30, 2015, from https://en.wikipedia.org/wiki/Sake

(71) Lewis, D. (2015, September 3). One Japanese company makes half of the world's zippers. Smithsonian. Retrieved January 15, 2016, from http://www.smithsonianmag.com/smart-news/one-japanese-company-makes-half-worlds-zippers-180956482/?no-ist

(72) Lewis, D. (2015, September 3). One Japanese company makes half of the world's zippers. Smithsonian. Retrieved January 15, 2016, from http://www.smithsonianmag.com/smart-news/one-japanese-company-makes-half-worlds-zippers-180956482/?no-ist

73) Smith, K. (2012, December 14). Why Japan is Obsessed with Kentucky Fried Chicken on Christmas. Retrieved December 30, 2015, from http://www.smithsonianmag.com/ist/?next=/arts-culture/why-japan-is-obsessed-with-kentucky-fried-chicken-on-christmas-1-161666960/

74) Cummings, T. (2010, March 18). Japan's strangest Kit Kat Flavors. Weird Asia News. Retrieved January 13, 2016, from http://www.weirdasianews.com/2010/03/18/japans-strangest-kit-kat-flavors/

75) Ivine, Dean (2 February 2013). "How did Kit Kat become king of candy in Japan?". CNN.com (Cable News Network). Retrieved 5 May 2013.

76) International availability of Fanta. (n.d.). Retrieved December 30, 2015, from https://en.wikipedia.org/wiki/International_availability_of_Fanta#pan

77) Raule, R. (2010, May 5). Top 10 Weirdest Japanese snacks and drinks. Top Tenz. Retrieved January 12, 2016, from http://www.toptenz.net/top-10-weirdest-japanese-snacks-and-drinks.php

78) Peterson, H. (2015, July 2). The secret strategy behind Burger King's black burgers in Japan. Business Insider. Retrieved December 29, 2015, from http://www.businessinsider.com/why-burger-king-japan-is-dying-its-burgers-black-2015-7

79) 50 McDonald's menu items only in Japan. (2014, July 7). Tsunagu Japan. Retrieved January 11, 2016, from https://www.tsunagujapan.com/50-mcdonalds-menu-items-only-in-japan/

80) Ashcraft, B. (2012, October 29). At McDonald's in Japan, French fries are causing all sorts of chaos. Kotaku.com. Retrieved January 14, 2016, from http://kotaku.com/5955694/at-mcdonalds-in-japan-french-fries-are-causing-all-sorts-of-chaos

1) Horse meat. (n.d.). Retrieved December 30, 2015, from https://en.wikipedia.org/wiki/Horse_meat#pan

2) Jha, A. (2011, September 30). Wasabi fire alarm scoops Ig Nobel prize for Japanese scientists. The Guardian. Retrieved January 12, 2016, from http://www.theguardian.com/science/2011/sep/30/wasabi-fire-alarm-ig-nobel-prize

3) Läsarnas sjuka varumärken". Dn.se. Retrieved January 13, 2016.

4) Bosrock, Mary Murray (September 2007). Asian Business Customs & Manners: A Country-by-Country Guide. Simon and Schuster. pp. 56–57. ISBN 978-0-684-05200-7. Retrieved July 13, 2015.

5) Gordenker, A. (2008, May 8). Anti-crime color balls. The Japan Times. Retrieved January 13, 2016, from http://www.japantimes.co.jp/news/2008/05/20/reference/anti-crime-color-balls/#.VpcGfPkrLIV

6) Nayar, Mandira. February 15. India, Japan and world peace. The Hindu (Chennai, India). Retrieved 11 November 2008.

7) Buerk, R. (2011, May 31). Japan pensioners volunteer to tackle nuclear crisis. BBC News. Retrieved January 13, 2016, from http://www.bbc.com/news/world-asia-pacific-13598607

) Duisen, M. (2013, September 9). The Weird Japanese Hole-In-One Tradition. Knowledgenuts. Retrieved January 14, 2016, from http://knowledgenuts.com/2013/09/09/the-weird-japanese-hole-in-one-tradition/

) Arita, E. (2010, February 28). Japan's love affair with dogs and cats. The Japan Times. Retrieved December 11, 2015.

) Erbland, K. (2013, October 30). Why are black cats considered bad luck? Mental Floss. Retrieved January 9, 2016, from http://mentalfloss.com/article/53397/why-are-black-cats-considered-bad-luck

) Left paw or right? Black, white or red? : Decoding the lucky cat. (2012, October 1). Retrieved January 9, 2016, from https://luckymaneko.wordpress.com

) Tama (cat). (n.d.). Retrieved May 19, 2015, from https://en.wikipedia.org/wiki/Tama_%28cat%29

) Hello Kitty is not a cat, plus more reveals before her L.A. tour". LA Times. August 26, 2014. Retrieved January 13, 2016.

) Ashcroft, Brian. Don't Be Silly, Hello Kitty Is a Cat. Retrieved January 13, 2016.

Cherry Blossom. (n.d.). Retrieved December 30, 2015, from https://en.wikipedia.org/wiki/Cherry_blossom

Choy Lee, Khoon. Japan—between Myth and Reality. 1995, page 142.

Cherry Blossom. (n.d.). Retrieved December 30, 2015, from https://en.wikipedia.org/wiki/Cherry_blossom

Cherry Blossom. (n.d.). Retrieved December 30, 2015, from https://en.wikipedia.org/wiki/Cherry_blossom

Koi. (n.d.). Retrieved December 30, 2015, from https://en.wikipedia.org/wiki/Koi

Yokohama Chinatown. (n.d.). Retrieved December 30, 2015, from https://en.wikipedia.org/wiki/Yokohama_Chinatown

) Japanese tea ceremony. (n.d.). Retrieved December 30, 2015, from https://en.wikipedia.org/wiki/Japanese_tea_ceremony

) Traditional Culture of Japan - Traditional crafts and culture. (n.d.). Retrieved January 13, 2016, from http://j-tradition.com/en/tea/history/.html

Japanese tea ceremony. (n.d.). Retrieved December 30, 2015, from https://en.wikipedia.org/wiki/Japanese_tea_ceremony

(108) (112) (169) Japan. (n.d.). Retrieved December 30, 2015, from https://en.wikipedia.org/wiki/Japan

Nikaido, Y. (2015, July 2). Japan's population decline the steepest on record. The Asahi Shimbun.

Israel, B. (2011, March 14). Japan's explosive geology explained. Livescience. Retrieved December 31, 2015, from http://www.livescience.com/30226-japan-tectonics-explosive-geology-ring-of-fire-110314.html

Tokyo. (n.d.). Retrieved December 30, 2015, from https://en.wikipedia.org/wiki/Tokyo

Japan. (n.d.). Retrieved December 30, 2015, from https://en.wikipedia.org/wiki/Japan

CIA Factbook: Japan". CIA.gov. Retrieved December 13, 2015.

(110) Barnes, Gina L. (2003). "Origins of the Japanese Islands" (PDF). University of Durham. Retrieved September 30, 2015.
(111) Kanamori, Shigenari (January 1, 1999). "German influences on Japanese Pre-War Constitution and Civil Code". European Journal of Law and Economics 7 (1): 93–95. doi:10.1023/A:1008688209052
(112) Japan. (n.d.). Retrieved December 30, 2015, from https://en.wikipedia.org/wiki/Japan
(113) Flag of Japan. (n.d.). Retrieved December 30, 2015, from https://en.wikipedia.org/wiki/Flag_of_Japan
(114) Flag of Japan. (n.d.). Retrieved December 30, 2015, from https://en.wikipedia.org/wiki/Flag_of_Japan
(115) Koh, Y. (2012, September 14). Japan Centenarian Population Tops 50,000. The Wall Street Journal (Blog). Retrieved December 31, 2015, from http://blogs.wsj.com/japanrealtime/2012/09/14/japan-centenarian-population-tops-50000/
(116) Nikaido, Y. (2015, July 2). Japan's population decline the steepest on record. The Asahi Shimbun.
(117) Harney, A. (2012, December 15). Without babies, can Japan survive? The New York Times. Retrieved December 12, 2015.
(118) Tokyo's 'oldest man' had been dead for 30 years. July 29, 2010. BBC News. Retrieved January 13, 2016, from http://www.bbc.com/news/world-asia-pacific-10809128
(119) Earth's day length shortened by Japan earthquake. CBS News. March 3 2011. Archived from the original on March 13 2011. Retrieved January 21 2016.
(120) Fackler, M. (2011, April 20). Tsunami warnings, written in stone. The New York Times. Retrieved January 2, 2016.
(121) CIA Factbook: Japan". CIA.gov. Retrieved December 13, 2015.
(122) Tsukiji fish market. (n.d.). Retrieved December 30, 2015, from https://en.wikipedia.org/wiki/Tsukiji_fish_market
(123) Tsukiji fish market. (n.d.). Retrieved December 30, 2015, from https://en.wikipedia.org/wiki/Tsukiji_fish_market
(124) Chiune Sugihara. (n.d.). Retrieved May 23, 2015, from https://en.wikipedia.org/wiki/Chiune_Sugihara
(125) Imperial regalia of Japan. (n.d.). Retrieved May 7, 2015, from https://en.wikipedia.org/wiki/Imperial_Regalia_of_Japan
(126) 1 Yen coin. (n.d.). Retrieved May 19, 2015, from https://en.wikipedia.org/wiki/1_yen_coin
(127) Ashiarai Yashiki. (n.d.). Villains Wikia. Retrieved January 14, 2016, from http://villains.wikia.com/wiki/Ashiarai_Yashiki
(128) Otter. Retrieved December 30, 2015, from https://en.wikipedia.org/wiki/Otter
(129) Moon rabbit. (n.d.). Retrieved December 30, 2015, from https://en.wikipedia.org/wiki/Moon_rabbit
(130) Mochi. (n.d.). Retrieved December 30, 2015, from https://en.wikipedia.org/wiki/Mochi
(131) Fujii, Y. (2013, December 5). UNESCO designates 'washoku' intangible cultural heritage asset. The Asahi Shimbun. Retrieved January 12 2016.
(132) Most expensive restaurant 2013: Kitcho, Kyoto eatery, chosen by daily meal. (2013, November 15). Huffington Post. Retrieved January 3, 2016, from http://www.huffingtonpost.ca/2013/11/15/kitcho-most-expensive-restaurant_n_4283224.html
(133) Bento. (n.d.). Retrieved December 30, 2015, from https://en.wikipedia.org/wiki/Bento
(134) Etiquette in Japan. (n.d.). Retrieved December 30, 2015, from https://en.wikipedia.org/wiki/Etiquette_in_Japan
(135) Sapporo Board of Education. Sapporo Bunko No.47. Hokkaidō News Bureau, 1998
(136) A mysterious and exciting night festival. Almost fully-naked men compete for good luck charms. (n.d.). Retrieved December 30, 2015, from http://www.jnto.go.jp/eng/location/spot/festival/saidaijieyohadaka.html
(137) Kanamara Matsuri 2014: What you should know about Japan's penis festival (NSFW PHOTOS). huffingtonpost.ca. Retrieved January 13 2016.
(138) Nuwer, R. (2013, October 4). This Japanese shrine has been torn down and rebuilt every 20 years for the past millennium. Smithsonian. com. Retrieved January 13, 2016, from http://www.smithsonianmag.com/smart-news/this-japanese-shrine-has-been-torn-down-and-rebuilt-every-20-years-for-the-past-millennium-575558/?no-ist (139) Caldwell, L. (2015, April 22). Japan's new maglev bullet train is now the fastest in the world. Slashgear. Retrieved December 30, 2015, from http://www.slashgear.com/japans-new-maglev-bullet-train-is-now-the-fastest-in-the-world-22380159/
(140) Mito, Y. (n.d.). Corporate culture as strong diving force for punctuality- another "Just in Time" Retrieved January 12, 2016, from https://web.archive.org/web/20081221165154/http://www.hitachi-rail.com.80/rail_now/column/just_in_time/index.html
(141) Shinjuku. (n.d.). Daisuki Japan. Retrieved January 3, 2016, from http://www.daisukijapan.com/guide/kanto/tokyo/shinjuku
(142) Heyden, T. (2014, November 19). Where is the world's best billboard site? BBC. Retrieved January 12, 2016, from http://www.bbc.com/news/magazine-30113027
(143) Haiku World's Shortest Form of Poetry. (2012, December 1). Kids Web Japan. Retrieved January 2, 2016, from http://web-japan.org/kidsweb/cool/12-12/
(144) Birmingham Museum of Art (2010). Birmingham Museum of Art : guide to the collection. [Birmingham, Ala]: Birmingham Museum of Art. p. 49. ISBN 978-1-904832-77-5.
(145) "Hoshi — The world's oldest hotel", Getaway Fact sheets, Ninemsn, September 21, 2006. Retrieved January 14, 2016.
(146) Toilets in Japan. (n.d.). Retrieved December 30, 2015, from https://en.wikipedia.org/wiki/Toilets_in_Japan
(147) Housing in Japan. (n.d.). Retrieved December 30, 2015, from https://en.wikipedia.org/wiki/Housing_in_Japan
(148) Wardell, Steven (October 1994), Capsule cure. Atlantic Monthly. 274 (4):42-47.
(149) Staples, Bill (2011). Kenichi Zenimura, Japanese American Baseball Pioneer. Jefferson, NC: McFarland. p. 15.
(150) (151) Baseball in Japan. (n.d.). Retrieved December 30, 2015, from https://en.wikipedia.org/wiki/Baseball_in_Japan
(152) Mike Snider (November 8, 2010). "Q&A: 'Mario' creator Shigeru Miyamoto". USA Today. Retrieved January 13, 2016.
(153) Plunkett, Luke (2010-09-13). "Happy 25th Birthday, Super Mario Bros.". Kotaku. Archived from the original on October 18, 2010. Retrieved January 13, 2016
(154) Nintendo. (n.d.). Retrieved December 30, 2015, from https://en.wikipedia.org/wiki/Nintendo
(155) Statistics - IFR International Federation of Robotics
(156) Karaoke. (n.d.). Retrieved December 30, 2015, from https://en.wikipedia.org/wiki/Karaoke
(157) Collinder, A. (2015, September 2). Japan ready to reclaim Blue Mountain coffee market. The Gleaner.
(158) Phipps, K. (2014, March 17). The Hidden Fortress. The Dissolve. Retrieved January 2, 2016, from https://thedissolve.com/reviews/644-the-hidden-fortress/
(159) Mochizuki, T. (2013, April 26). Japan and Russia move closer as both eye China. The Wall Street Journal. Retrieved January 12, 2016.
(160) Mr Kanso: The restaurant where everything comes in a tin. (2015, March 10). Retrieved December 30, 2015, from http://www.news.co au/lifestyle/food/restaurants-bars/mr-kanso-the-restaurant-where-everything-comes-in-a-tin/news-story/4f9b03c41be2c1fbca89aacbe701713
(161) Dennō Senshi Porygon. (n.d.). Retrieved December 28, 2015, from https://en.wikipedia.org/wiki/Dennō_Senshi_Porygon
(162) Mulhern, S. (2015, March 29). If you want to live in Miyakejima, Japan you must carry a gas mask at all times. The Plaid Zebra.
(163) Coldwell, W. (2014, June 2). Rabbit Island: A Japanese holiday resort for bunnies. The Guardian. Retrieved December 29, 2015, from http://www.theguardian.com/travel/2014/jun/02/rabbit-island-okunoshima-japan-holiday-resort-bunnies
(164) Japan, Brazil mark a century of settlement, family ties. The Japan Times Online. Retrieved 2015-11-02.

(165) Etiquette in Japan. Retrieved December 30, 2015, from https://en.wikipedia.org/wiki/Etiquette_in_Japan

(166) How (and why) square watermelons are made - what about watermelon? (2009, July 13). Whataboutwatermellon.com. Retrieved December 31, 2015, from http://www.whataboutwatermelon.com/index.php/2009/07/how-and-why-square-watermelons-are-made/

(167) Buerk, R. (March 15, 2012). Japan's obsession with perfect fruit. BBC News. Retrieved January 5, 2016, from http://www.bbc.com/news/world-radio-and-tv-17352173

(168) Nakagawa, Dai; Matsunaka, Ryoji (2006). Transport Policy and Funding. Elsevier. p. 63. ISBN 0-08-044852-6.

(169) Japan. (n.d.). Retrieved December 30, 2015, from https://en.wikipedia.org/wiki/Japan

(170) Japan. (n.d.). Retrieved December 30, 2015, from https://en.wikipedia.org/wiki/Japan

(171) H, L. (2013, April 3). MT. Mihara – The Most Depressing Volcano in the World. Exciting Earth. Retrieved 2016, from https://excitingearth.wordpress.com/2013/04/03/MT.-mihara-the-most-depressing-volcano-in-the-world/

(172) MT. Mihara. (n.d.). Retrieved December 30, 2015, from https://en.wikipedia.org/wiki/MT._Mihara

(173) Lambe, S. (2014, May 13). All the cities destroyed by Godzilla. VH1. Retrieved January 3, 2016, from http://www.vh1.com/news/87514/cities-destroyed-by-godzilla/

(174) Chen, H. (2015, June 3). Godzilla finally gets citizenship in Japan. BBC News. Retrieved 2016, from http://www.bbc.com/news/world-asia-32987622

(175) WKF claims 100 million practitioners. Thekisontheway.com. Retrieved September 3, 2015.

(176) History of Shotokan (Russian). Retrieved November 5, 2015.

(177) Karate. (n.d.). Retrieved December 30, 2015, from https://en.wikipedia.org/wiki/Karate

(178) Bolton, D. (2015, June 23). Japan finally lifts its 67-year-old ban on dancing. Independent. Retrieved December 28, 2015, from http://www.independent.co.uk/news/world/asia/japan-finally-lifts-its-67-year-old-ban-on-dancing-10340816.html

(179) Holloway, A. (2015, September 5). Kongo gumi: Oldest continuously operating company survives 1,400 years before crash. Ancient Origins. Retrieved December 31, 2015, from http://www.ancient-origins.net/history/kongo-gumi-oldest-continuously-operating-company-survives-1400-years-crash-003765

(180) Wilks, J. (2011, August 25). Tokyo facts: 40 trivia tidbits to wow your mind. Time Out. Retrieved January 2, 2016, from http://www.timeout.com/tokyo/things-to-do/tokyo-facts-40-trivia-tidbits-to-wow-your-mind

(181) Guns N' Roses Plays Longest Concert Ever In Tokyo. Roadrunnerrecords.com. Retrieved June 19, 2015..

(182) Spacey, J. (2014, March 14). Doomed swan boat lovers (Japanese urban legend). Japan Talk. Retrieved January 3, 2016, from http://www.japan-talk.com/jt/new/inokashira-park-urban-legend

(183) Vending Machines. (n.d.). Retrieved December 28, 2015, from http://www.jnto.go.jp/eng/indepth/cultural/hj/vendingmachines.html

(184) Kichi, D. (2014, April 24). 25 things you'll only find in vending machines in Japan. Retrieved December 28, 2015, from http://www.doramafever.com/news/25-things-youll-only-find-in-vending-machines-in-japan/

(185) Kaplan, D.; Dubro, A: Yakuza, page 14. University of California Press, 2003.

(186) Japanorama, BBC Three, Series 2, Episode 3, first aired September 21, 2006.

(187) Tokyo. (n.d.). Retrieved December 30, 2015, from https://en.wikipedia.org/wiki/Tokyo

(188) Junihotoe. (n.d.). Retrieved December 30, 2015, from https://en.wikipedia.org/wiki/Junihotoe

(189) Ohaguro. (n.d.). Retrieved December 30, 2015, from https://en.wikipedia.org/wiki/Ohaguro

(190) Kobe Beef. (n.d.). Retrieved January 11, 2016, from http://www.foodreference.com/html/artkobebeef.html

(191) Whisky for everyone. (n.d.). Retrieved January 11, 2016, from http://www.whiskyforeveryone.com/whisky_regions/japan.html

(192) Cosme, S. (2013, August 6). 10 Things you need to know about Japanese whisky. Complex. Retrieved January 13, 2016, from http://www.complex.com/pop-culture/2013/08/facts-about-japanese-whisky/the-highball-is-king-in-japan

(193) Schneider, K. (2014, January 9). Are these the most outrageous hotel designs ever? News.com.au. Retrieved January 13, 2016.

(194) Wojnowski, T. (2013, March 1). World's Shortest Escalator - Kanagawa - Japan Travel - Tourism Guide, Japan Map and Trip Planner. Retrieved December 28, 2015, from

(195) The lost generation of Japanese Internet cafe kids. (2011, November 12). Retrieved January 14, 2016, from http://www.japan-talk.com/jt/new/the-lost-generation-of-Japanese-internet-cafe-kids

(196) MacGregor, H. (1996, January 30). Japanese are crazy for comics. Los Angeles Times. Retrieved 2016.

(197) List of best-selling manga. (n.d.). Retrieved December 30, 2015, from https://en.wikipedia.org/wiki/List_of_best-selling_manga

(198) Terumitsu Otsu and Mary Kennard (April 27, 2002). "The art of voice acting". The Daily Yomiuri. p. 11.

(199) Hachiko. (n.d.). Retrieved December 30, 2015, from https://en.wikipedia.org/wiki/Hachiko

(200) "Hachiko, Japan's most loyal dog, finally reunited with owner in heartwarming new statue in Tokyo". rocketnews24.com. February 2015. Retrieved December 21, 2015.

(201) Farrar, L. (2009, February 26). Cell phone stories writing new chapter in print publishing. CNN. Retrieved January 10, 2016, from http://edition.cnn.com/2009/TECH/02/25/japan.mobilenovels/

(202) Simonitch, S. (2012, October 3). Japan Today. Retrieved January 9, 2016, from http://www.japantoday.com/category/lifestyle/view/japans-cat-cuddle-cafe-lets-you-sleep-with-a-stranger-for-y6000-an-hour

(203) The many ways to say sorry in Japanese. (2015, August 14). BBC. Retrieved January 10, 2016, from http://www.bbc.com/news/world-33901966

(204) Ao (Color). (n.d.). Retrieved December 30, 2015, from https://en.wikipedia.org/wiki/Ao_(color)

(205) Etiquette in Japan. Retrieved December 30, 2015, from https://en.wikipedia.org/wiki/Etiquette_in_Japan

(206) Bosrock, Mary Murray (September 2007). Asian Business Customs & Manners: A Country-by-Country Guide. Simon and Schuster. pp. 57. ISBN 978-0-684-05200-7. Retrieved July 13, 2015.

(207) Yamaguchi, Mari. February 1, 2009. In Japan, Your Blood Type Says It All. Huffington Post. Retrieved January 14, 2016.

(208) Sapa (October 4, 2004). "Sound Princess eliminates toilet noises" (http). IOL. Retrieved January 14, 2016

(209) Szczepanski, K. (2014, December 16). Learn about the four-tiered class system of feudal Japan. About.com. Retrieved January 14, 2016, from http://asianhistory.about.com/od/japan/p/ShogJapanClass.htm

(210) Atomic bombings of Hiroshima and Nagasaki. (n.d.). Retrieved May 19, 2015, from https://en.wikipedia.org/wiki/Atomic_bombings_of_shima_and_Nagasaki#Double_survivors

(211) Japanese writing system. (n.d.). Retrieved December 30, 2015, from https://en.wikipedia.org/wiki/Japanese_writing_system

(212) Toyota. (n.d.). Retrieved December 30, 2015, from https://en.wikipedia.org/wiki/Toyota

(213) Japanese macaque. (n.d.). Retrieved December 30, 2015, from https://en.wikipedia.org/wiki/Japanese_macaque

(214) Japanese New Year. (n.d.). Retrieved December 30, 2015, from https://en.wikipedia.org/wiki/Japanese_New_Year

(215) Sokushinbutsu. (n.d.). Retrieved May 19, 2015, from https://en.wikipedia.org/wiki/Sokushinbutsu

(216) Japanese garden. (n.d.). Retrieved December 30, 2015, from https://en.wikipedia.org/wiki/Japanese_garden#Karesansui_dry_rock_gardens

(217) Shelley, Rex, Teo Chuu Tong, and Jacqueline Ong. 2012. Japan (Cultures of the World, Third). Tarrytown, NY: Marshall Cavendish.

(218) Ernst, E. (1956). The Kabuki Theatre, pp.10-12. New York: Oxford University Press.

(219) Kabuki. (n.d.). Retrieved December 30, 2015, from https://en.wikipedia.org/wiki/Kabuki

(220) Kelly, Jason M. (2012). "Why Did Henry Stimson Spare Kyoto from the Bomb?: Confusion in Postwar Historiography". Journal of American-East Asian Relations 19: 183–203. doi:10.1163/18765610-01902004.

(221) Lee, Jennifer 8. (January 16, 2008). Solving a Riddle Wrapped in a Mystery Inside a Cookie. The New York Times. Retrieved on January 16, 2008.